Cambridge **Discovery Education**™

▶ **INTERACTIVE READERS**

Series editor: Bob Hastings

THE TRADITIONS OF DEATH

B1+

Brian Sargent

CAMBRIDGE UNIVERSITY PRESS
Cambridge, New York, Melbourne, Madrid, Cape Town,
Singapore, São Paulo, Delhi, Mexico City

Cambridge University Press
32 Avenue of the Americas, New York, NY 10013-2473, USA

www.cambridge.org
Information on this title: www.cambridge.org/9781107635784

First published 2014

Printed in Hong Kong, China, by Golden Cup Printing Company Limited

A catalog record for this publication is available from the British Library.

Library of Congress Cataloging-in-Publication Data

Sargent, Brian, 1969-
  The traditions of death / Brian Sargent.
    pages cm. -- (Cambridge discovery interactive readers)
  ISBN 978-1-107-63578-4 (pbk. : alk. paper)
  1. Funeral rites and ceremonies--Juvenile literature. 2. English language--Textbooks for foreign
speakers. 3. Readers (Elementary) I. Title.

GT3150.S37 2013
393'.93--dc23

                    2013024751

ISBN 978-1-107-63578-4

Additional resources for this publication at www.cambridge.org

Art direction, book design, and photo research: Q2A/Bill Smith
Layout services: Q2A/Bill Smith
Editorial services: hyphen S.A.
Audio production: Q2A/Bill Smith

Contents

Before You Read:
Get Ready!

Sooner or later it happens to everyone: death. In this book, we look at the causes of death, what people have believed about death, and how people have behaved around death in both the past and the present.

Words to Know

Look at the pictures. Then complete the paragraph below with the correct form of the highlighted words.

A cemetery with gravestones

A funeral around a coffin

Mourners visiting the grave of a loved one

In many countries when someone dies, people take the body to a
❶ _____ . There they have a ceremony called a
❷ _____ . The ❸ _____ stand
and watch as the ❹ _____ is lowered into the
❺ _____ . The date of the person's birth and death are
written on the ❻ _____ .

Words to Know

Read the paragraph. Write the correct form of the highlighted words next to their definitions below.

Ancient cultures had different views on death. Ancient Egyptians believed souls would return to their bodies after death. They preserved the bodies of their dead by making them into mummies. Ancient Aztecs believed their gods ate human hearts. They sacrificed large numbers of people to feed their gods. During the ritual, they took the hearts from their sacrifices and burned them to ashes.

1 _____ : the soft, gray stuff left after something has burned

2 _____ : a set of actions always done the same way at the same time, sometimes as part of a religion

3 _____ : the part of a person not in the body but that some people believe continues to live after the body dies

4 _____ : kill to please a god in a religious ceremony, or the act of killing

5 _____ : a body that has been dried

6 _____ : keep something the same for a long time

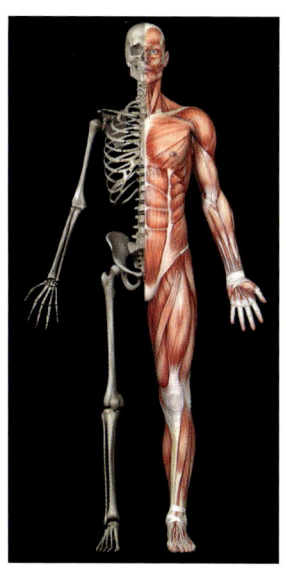

SCIENCE CORNER

The bones that make up a body are called the skeleton. The body moves when muscles pull and push the bones of the skeleton. Often, disease or illness can hurt or even kill the body.

CHAPTER 1

Going out with a Bang

ONE MAN WAS REMEMBERED AS HE HAD LIVED.

For most of the year, Meredith Smith of Indiana, USA, worked in a school. He took care of the school building and repaired things that were broken. However, every summer, Mr. Smith was also a pyrotechnician – someone who works with fireworks.

For nearly 40 years, Mr. Smith ran a fireworks show in his neighborhood. The show was to celebrate the Fourth of July, Independence Day in the United States. It was one of his favorite things to do. Some years, when the neighborhood didn't have enough money for the show, he paid for it himself.

Mr. Smith died in 2008. To remember him, that year's show had one special firework. It was bright white and shone in the night sky when it exploded at the very end of the show. Inside it were some of Mr. Smith's **ashes**.

Death is a part of human life, but different cultures have very different views about it. To some, death is a sad event. Many cultures have **rituals** that allow the living to feel sadness over the death of a relative or close friend. This time of **mourning** may be many months or even years. In 19th-century England, a widow[1] was expected to **mourn** as long as two years.

Other cultures see death as a time of celebration. In these cultures, people have parties or even festivals to celebrate the person's life, not mourn his or her death. The people close to Meredith Smith saw death as both a time of mourning and a time of celebration. They were sad that he had died, but making his ashes part of a fireworks show was the perfect way to celebrate his life. A friend of Mr. Smith's told the newspapers, "I can't think of a better way."

[1] **widow:** a woman whose husband has died

? UNDERSTAND

What did Meredith Smith's family and friends do to remember him? Why?

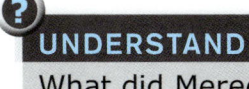

CHAPTER 2

The Power of Death

MANY PEOPLE BELIEVE DEATH HAS A MYSTERIOUS POWER.

There is an Indonesian myth[2] about the power of death. The people in this myth, Joko Seger and Princess Roro Anteng, were a couple that could not have any children. One day, Joko Seger received a message from the gods. They said he and Princess Roro would have 25 children if they agreed to do one thing. They had to **sacrifice** their last child. They had to take the child to the top of Mount Bromo, a nearby volcano, and throw the child inside.

When the time came, if they didn't make the **sacrifice**, Mount Bromo would erupt[3] and destroy all the land around it.

Joko Seger agreed, and soon he and Princess Roro had their first child.

[2]**myth:** an ancient story about gods and brave people, often one that explains the natural world
[3]**erupt:** When a volcano erupts, it throws out smoke, fire, ashes, and rocks.

Twenty-five children later, it was time for the couple to make the sacrifice and kill their youngest child, but they couldn't do it. The gods sent an earthquake[4] to remind the couple of their promise. Finally, in a big ceremony, Joko Seger and Princess Roro Anteng threw their youngest child, Kesuma, into Mount Bromo, and the gods were pleased.

Interestingly, although this story is only a myth, the sacrifices at Mount Bromo continue today. Every year there is a festival, and people come from far away to throw food, money, and animals into the volcano. Sometimes, local people climb inside the volcano and try to catch the sacrifices as they are thrown inside. Happily, child sacrifices are not part of the modern festival.

People climb inside the Mount Bromo volcano to catch sacrifices.

In some places, human sacrifice still exists, but it is extremely uncommon. Animal sacrifices, however, continue in many parts of the modern world.

[4] **earthquake:** a sudden movement of the Earth

? EVALUATE

Many people are against sacrificing animals. Should it be allowed?

As in the Indonesian myth, sacrifices are usually made to a god. In ancient times, human and animal sacrifices were common. For example, farmers often gave the gods sacrifices, hoping it would make their farms successful. In ancient Greece, the *hecatomb* was a sacrifice of 100 cows to please the gods Apollo, Athena, and Hera. Over 700 years ago, the Chimú people of Peru sacrificed nearly 200 people to the sea god, Ni, for success in war.

Of course, not all sacrifices happened in the past. The Gadhimai festival in Nepal is a yearly celebration that includes animal sacrifices. Over 200,000 animals are sacrificed each year during the two-day festival.

People make the sacrifices hoping the gods will grant their wishes[5] or to thank the gods for granting their wishes. Thousands of people attend the festival every year, some coming from other countries.

India, like many places, has a history of human sacrifices. Today, they are extremely uncommon, but sometimes they do still happen. In 2012, a woman in a small village in India was looking for her missing daughter. She was told by a *tantric*, or religious person, to sacrifice a young boy from the village, and her daughter would return to her. She took her neighbor's seven-year-old son, hit him with stones, then threw him down a well.[6] Amazingly, the boy lived and was rescued by a local farmer. The woman and the tantric were both arrested.

[5] **grant a wish:** make something you hope for come true
[6] **well:** a deep hole in the ground from which you can get water

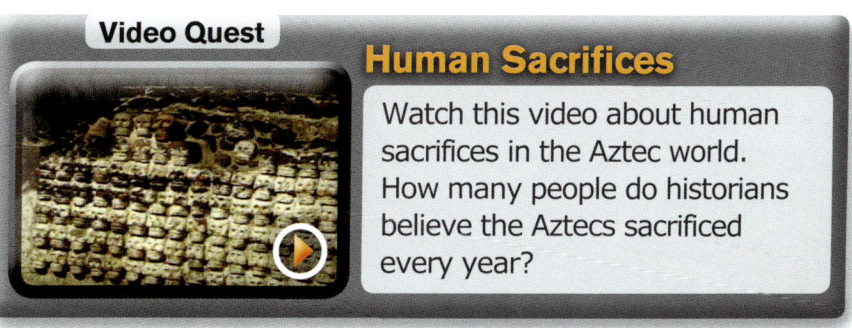

Video Quest

Human Sacrifices

Watch this video about human sacrifices in the Aztec world. How many people do historians believe the Aztecs sacrificed every year?

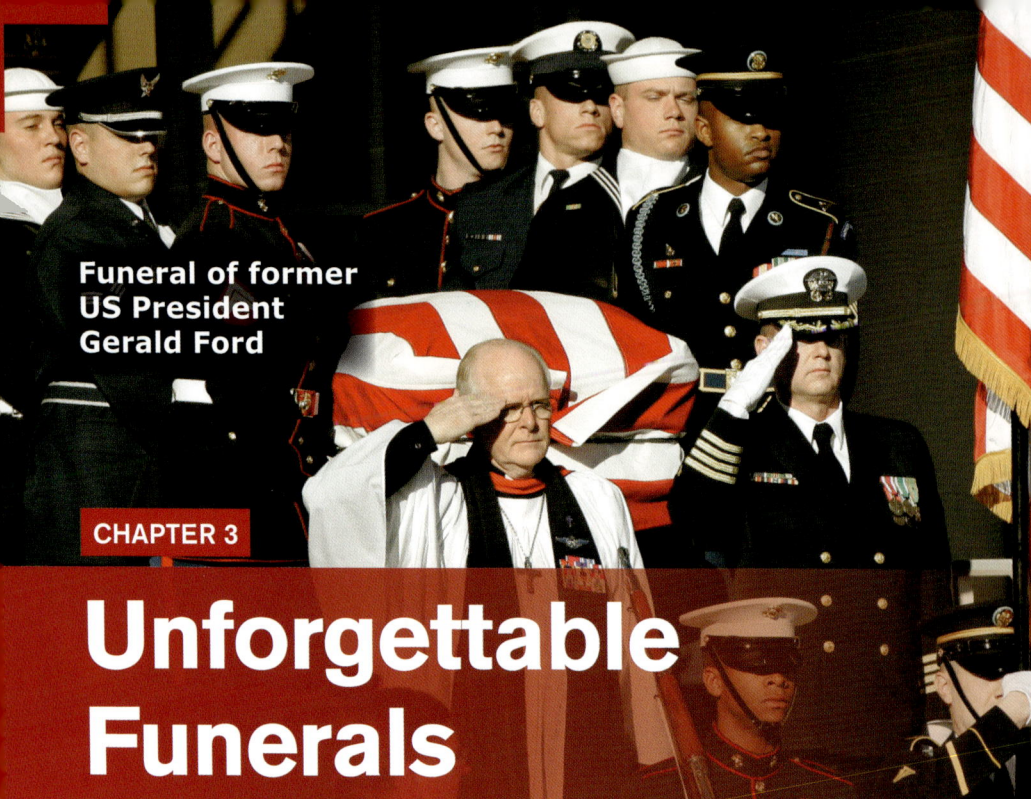

Funeral of former
US President
Gerald Ford

CHAPTER 3

Unforgettable Funerals

SOME FAMOUS FUNERALS ARE TOO STRANGE TO BE BELIEVED.

All people die. It does not matter if they are rich or poor, everyone dies sooner or later. However, that doesn't mean everyone's **funeral** will be the same.

Funerals in the United States are not usually very loud. Traditionally, they begin in a house of worship[7] and continue to a **cemetery** where the body is **buried** in the ground. Although religious songs are often sung, American funerals are peaceful, quiet events.

[7]**house of worship:** where religious ceremonies take place

So in 1932, the townspeople of Sallisaw, Oklahoma, were surprised when around 20,000 people came to see the funeral of Charles A. Floyd. The people were neither quiet nor respectful.[8] Some sat in chairs meant for Floyd's family. Others stood on top of gravestones to watch. During the funeral some people ate food and others shouted out rude words.

Charles Floyd was better known as "Pretty Boy Floyd," a handsome man who was also a bank robber and murderer. Newspapers around the country had made Pretty Boy Floyd famous. Many people came to his funeral for a chance to see his body in the coffin before it was buried.

For years afterward, people visiting Floyd's grave would steal things from the small cemetery to keep as a memory. In 1985, even Floyd's gravestone was stolen.

Though Pretty Boy Floyd's funeral was the largest in Oklahoma, it was very small compared to the funeral of C. N. Annadurai. Annadurai was the very popular head of the South Indian state of Tamil Nadu. When he died in 1969, 15 million people came to his funeral. It still holds the record for the largest funeral in history.

[8] **respectful:** show with your behavior that something is important or valuable

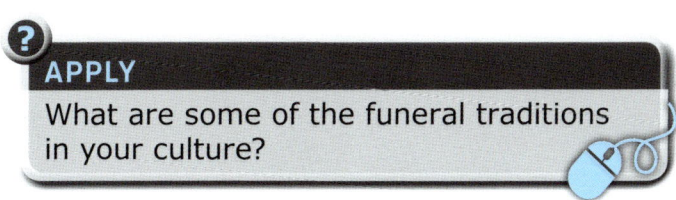

? APPLY

What are some of the funeral traditions in your culture?

Not everyone can have millions of people come to their funeral, but what about millions of people coming to their grave? That is what happens at the amazing pyramids of Egypt. The pyramids were built as tombs – or special houses for the dead – for the *pharaohs*, the kings of ancient Egypt.

Most tombs are built after the person dies, but the pharaohs wanted to make sure their tombs were very special. So, they began building them as soon as they became pharaohs. The largest of Egypt's pyramids, the Great Pyramid of Giza, was begun by the Pharaoh Khufu nearly 5,000 years ago. It is made of about two million stone blocks and took as long as 30 years to build.

Khufu's body was mummified and placed deep inside the pyramid. Mummification was common in ancient Egypt. Bodies were dried, then wrapped in cloth to preserve them.

Mummies are wrapped in cloth.

Egyptians believed that bodies should be preserved because, after death, the soul of a person would return to the body. To return, the soul had to recognize the body. Masks[9] that look like the dead person were sometimes placed over the face and body to help each soul find the right body.

Mummies have been found in other places around the world; in the Americas as well as Europe and Asia. One of the strangest mummification traditions comes from Japan: self-mummification, a very uncommon Japanese Buddhist tradition.

Buddhists monks[10] wanting to self-mummify would dry their bodies while still alive. For several years, they ate very little and drank a special poisonous[11] tea. This process took a long time and ended with the person entering their own tomb while still alive, then sitting still until he died. Self-mummification has been against the law since the early 1900s. But today, these mummies are still shown to religious visitors and tourists.

A self-mummified monk

[9] **mask:** a cover for the face that hides or decorates it
[10] **monk:** a man who lives in a religious group apart from other people
[11] **poisonous:** able to cause illness or death

After the funeral, the Tana Toraja people take their dead to a final resting place.

Funerals are very important in the Tana Toraja area of Indonesia, so important that each person gets two!

The first funeral is a small event, held just after the person dies. The second funeral takes place much later, after the family has saved enough money to hold a huge public party.

Second funerals take a lot of money in Tana Toraja. While the family is saving money for the party, they keep the person's body, often under the family's house. It can take several years to save enough money!

Sometimes thousands of guests attend the funeral party, which can last for many days. Even tourists are welcome. Guests give the family presents such as animals, food, and drink. Then a number of animals are killed, and the meat is given to the guests. For larger parties, the animal sacrifices can go on all day without breaks.

At the end of the celebration, the body is moved to its final resting place. The people of Tana Toraja place their dead in caves in nearby cliffs or in coffins tied with rope to the side of a mountain.

These coffins are tied to the side of a mountain with ropes.

It may be unusual for a dead person to stay with the family until they can afford a big party, but the Malagasy people in Madagascar also spend a lot of time with their dead. Every seven years, the families dig up their dead relatives and dance with them.

The ceremony, called *Famadihana*, which means the Turning of the Bones, is a way for families to show respect and love to those who have died. Before dancing through the streets, the families wrap the bodies in new, fresh cloth and sometimes spray them with expensive perfume.

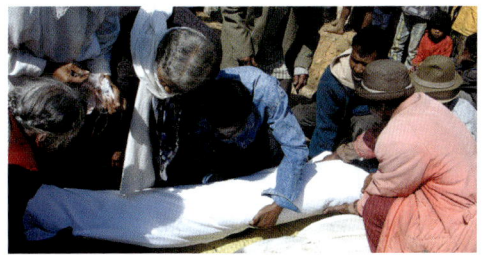

The Malagasy wrap their dead in new cloth every seven years.

Video Quest

Day of the Dead

Watch this video to learn about a celebration in Mexico. What do children in Mexico do during the celebration?

CHAPTER 4

Solving the Mystery of Death

WHY DO ALL LIVING THINGS DIE?

In 1513, Spanish explorer Ponce de Leon traveled to Florida. Many say he was looking for the Fountain of Youth – a magical fountain whose waters will keep you alive forever. Of course, Ponce de Leon did not find this fountain, but he was not the only one to look for it. Many people have searched for this magical cure for death. It is easy to see why. Nobody wants to get old and die.

Why do people die of old age? This is a surprisingly hard question to answer. The parts of the human body only work for a certain time. As the body ages, bones break more easily. Muscles, including the heart, become weaker. Eventually, the body stops working and we die. Scientists and doctors know this happens, but they do not agree on why.

For years, scientists believed damage to our bodies was the reason. Damage because of time and illness builds up in the body. As the body becomes more and more damaged, it is less able to repair itself, until – finally – death comes.

It is possible, however, that the reason we age and die is not so much because of the damage our bodies suffer but because of our **genes**. Genes are the parts of our cells[12] that tell the cell what to do. Some scientists believe our genes may be telling the body when it is time to die.

Scientists studying a kind of worm[13] found something very interesting. By changing only a single gene in the worm, they caused it to live twice as long as usual.

Have these scientists found the Fountain of Youth? Will they find a gene in humans that allows us to live twice as long? Most of us hope they can answer this question quickly!

....
[12]**cell:** the smallest living part of an animal or a plant
[13]**worm:** a small creature with a long, thin, soft body and no legs

Of course, old age is only one possible cause of death. By looking closely at other causes, we can learn what we must do to live longer. Researchers[14] collect information on deaths around the world. The information helps them decide what should be done to help people live longer.

In one case, researchers found that the most common cause of death around the world was **disease**. Looking closer, they found the type of disease depended upon how much money the country had.

In high-income[15] countries, the most common causes of death are non-contagious diseases. These are diseases such as heart disease or cancer that cannot go from one person to another.

In low-income countries, however, contagious diseases are the most common cause of death. These are diseases such as tuberculosis, HIV, and malaria. The researchers share this information to help people and governments know the best way to fight the causes of death in their area.

[14] **researcher:** someone who studies a subject in detail to learn new information about it

[15] **income:** the money you earn by working

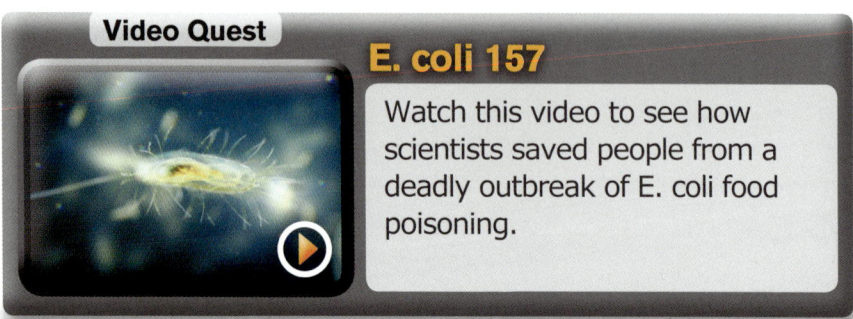

Video Quest

E. coli 157

Watch this video to see how scientists saved people from a deadly outbreak of E. coli food poisoning.

A forensic scientist studies skulls and other bones.

In addition to solving the mystery of worldwide deaths, science can help solve the mystery of single deaths. In many cases, death leaves behind almost nothing, perhaps just a skeleton. When that skeleton is found, it is up to doctors and scientists to find out what happened to the person.

To a regular person, all skeletons look alike. However, forensic scientists are trained to see things that regular people cannot. They can tell the age of a skeleton and whether it is male or female. Looking at the skeleton, they can see the health of the person, where the person's family is from, and even how the person died.

One famous death solved by scientists was the death of Ötzi, the Iceman. Nobody knows much about Ötzi. We don't even know his real name. He's called Ötzi because in 1991, his body was found in the Ötztal Alps, mountains between Austria and Italy. He'd been frozen there for over 5,000 years.

Today, Ötzi is still frozen. He is kept in Italy in a freezer at exactly –6°C, and scientists are studying his body to see what they can learn about this mysterious man. From his bones, they learned he was about 45 years old and came from a valley nearby, though he spent most of his time in the mountains. From his mummified skin, they learned he had tattoos.[16] From his genes, they learned he had brown hair and brown eyes.

Research on Ötzi is very slow. He spends most of his time frozen, and he is rarely warmed up enough to be studied. Perhaps that is why no one found the arrowhead in his left shoulder until 2001.

[16] **tattoo:** a design on a person's skin that does not come off

Ötzi the Iceman was murdered! The oldest natural mummy in the world is also one of the world's oldest unsolved crimes!

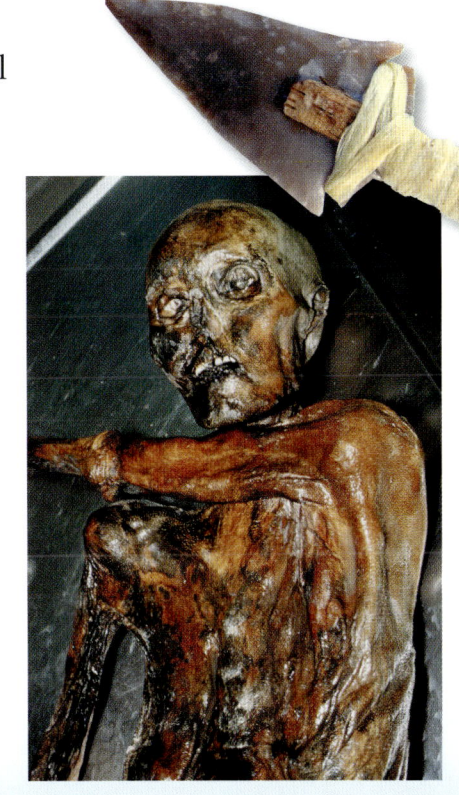

Ötzi was shot in the back and died soon after. It is not clear why he was killed or who did it. Scientists know it was springtime when Ötzi died, but the killer left the body in the mountains to be covered by the snows of winter. Now, 5,000 years later, scientists continue to look closely at this man to understand more about both his life and death.

The Iceman was found with an arrowhead in his shoulder.

CHAPTER 5

What Do You Think?

GHANA IS A LAND OF JUNGLES AND BEACHES – AND FANTASTIC COFFINS.

Ata Owoo is a carpenter[17] who lives in the West African country of Ghana. Sometime in the 1950s, Mr. Owoo made a beautiful chair in the shape of a large bird, an eagle. The chair was for a local village leader, or chief. Mr. Owoo designed it to be carried on the shoulders of the chief's villagers.

The eagle chair was so amazing, another village chief asked for a chair of his own. He wanted it to look like a cocoa pod, a common crop[18] from the area. However, the chief died before Mr. Owoo could finish the chair. When Mr. Owoo heard the news, he turned the cocoa pod chair into a coffin for the chief. Mr. Owoo did not know it, but he had just changed funerals in Ghana forever.

[17] **carpenter:** a person whose job is making wooden objects

[18] **crop:** a plant that is grown by farmers

Sixty years later, funerals in Ghana are famous for fantastic coffins. They come in every possible shape and size. There are coffins in the shape of food, animals, cars, airplanes, shoes, even ice cream. Usually the coffins show something about the personality or the job of the person to be buried. The coffins are now very popular. Mr. Owoo and others even make them for people from other countries.

What do you think? How would you feel if you attended the funeral of someone buried in a coffin that looked like a cell-phone? Or a snake?

If it were your funeral, what shape of coffin would you like? What shape would show your personality? Your job? Can you think of a coffin shape that would most surprise your family? Each coffin takes about three months to build, so don't wait too long to decide!

After You Read

Correctly complete each sentence by choosing Ⓐ, Ⓑ, Ⓒ, or Ⓓ.

1 The record for the largest funeral in history is _____ .

Ⓐ the funeral of Charles "Pretty Boy" Floyd

Ⓑ the funeral of C.N. Annadurai

Ⓒ the funeral of Ötzi the Iceman

Ⓓ the funeral of Ata Owoo

2 The Great Pyramid of Giza is _____ .

Ⓐ where an Egyptian Pharaoh once lived

Ⓑ an Egyptian cemetery

Ⓒ the tomb of the Pharaoh Khufu

Ⓓ the tomb of many pharoahs

3 The "Turning of the Bones" happens _____ .

Ⓐ every seven years in Madagascar

Ⓑ on Independence Day in the United States

Ⓒ every year in Ghana

Ⓓ at the Mount Bromo volcano in Indonesia

4 The most common cause of death in high-income countries is _____ .

Ⓐ contagious disease

Ⓑ non-contagious disease

Ⓒ accidents

Ⓓ self-mummification

5 A cocoa pod was the design for _____ .

Ⓐ the fountain of youth

Ⓑ a Day of the Dead doll

Ⓒ a new kind of gene

Ⓓ a coffin in Ghana

True or False?

Read the sentences and choose Ⓐ (True) or Ⓑ (False).

❶ Every year, people visit Mount Bromo and throw sacrifices into the volcano.

Ⓐ True

Ⓑ False

❷ The people of the Tana Toraja area of Indonesia bring out their dead every year and dance with them.

Ⓐ True

Ⓑ False

❸ Ötzi the Iceman was killed by an arrow.

Ⓐ True

Ⓑ False

❹ The first coffin Mr. Owoo created was in the shape of an eagle.

Ⓐ True

Ⓑ False

Complete the Sentences

Use the words in the box to complete the sentences.

ashes	funeral	grave	mummy	tomb

❶ The Great Pyramid of Giza is a _____ for the Egyptian Pharaoh Khufu.

❷ Mrs. Johnson goes to the cemetery to visit her husband's _____ every Tuesday.

❸ Bobby was too young to remember his great grandmother, but he does remember attending her _____ .

❹ Scientists have to be very careful when unwrapping the _____ because it's 3,000 years old.

❺ After the coffin was burned, only _____ were left.

Answer Key

Words to Know, page 4
1 cemetery **2** funeral **3** mourners **4** coffin **5** grave
6 gravestone

Words to Know, page 5
1 ashes **2** ritual **3** soul **4** sacrifice **5** mummy
6 preserve

Understand, page 7
They held a special fireworks show and put some of his ashes in the last one.

Evaluate, page 9   *Answers will vary.*

Video Quest, page 11
Historians believe that the Aztecs sacrificed about 30,000 people every year.

Apply, page 13   *Answers will vary.*

Video Quest, page 17
The children in Mexico decorate and eat skulls made of sugar, called *calaveras de azúcar*, during the Day of the Dead celebration.

Video Quest, page 20
Investigators made a list of possible foods and interviewed people to see which foods may have contained E. coli.

Choose the Correct Answers, page 26
1 B **2** C **3** A **4** B **5** D

True or False?, page 27
1 A **2** B **3** A **4** B

Complete the Sentences, page 27
1 tomb **2** grave **3** funeral **4** mummy **5** ashes